GW00706073

¡Fantástico!

A Little Book of Spanish

LIVING LANGUAGE®
A RANDOM HOUSE COMPANY

Living Language books and packages are available at special discounts for bulk purchases for premiums and sales promotions, as well as for fund-raising or educational use. For more information contact the Special Sales Manager at the address below.

Published by Living Language, A Random House Company,
280 Park Avenue, New York, New York 10017.
Living Language is a member of the Random House
Information Group.

Random House, Inc. New York, Toronto, London, Sydney, Auckland
www.livinglanguage.com

Living Language and colophon are registered trademarks of
Random House, Inc.

Printed in Singapore
Designed by Blue Farm Bookworks
Library of Congress Cataloguing in Publication Data is
available upon request.

ISBN 0-609-60617-4

10 9 8 7 6 5 4 3 2

First Edition

There's only one thing better than saying the right thing at the right time, and that's doing it in a foreign language. *¡Fantastico! A Little Book of Spanish* will introduce a little sophistication, savvy, and *savoir faire* into your next conversation. Whether you want to dispense age-old wisdom like "You're making an elephant out of a flea!" or just want to say "Bless you," after someone sneezes, *¡Fantastico!* will get you noticed!

¡Fantástico!

A Little Book of Spanish

What's new?

¿Qué hay de nuevo?

[keh EYE deh NWEH-voh]

Fantastic!

¡Fantástico!

[fahn-TAHS-tee-koh]

No way!

¡Ni loco!

[nee LOH-koh]

I don't think so.

Me late que no.

[meh LAH-teh keh NOH]

(lit: My heart beat tells me no.)

Isn't it a little late
for that?

¿A estas alturas?

[ah EHS-tahs ahl-TOO-rahs]

(lit: At these heights?)

My God!

¡Dios mío!

[DYOHS MEE-oh]

Out of sight, out of mind

Ojos que no ven, corazón que no siente.

[OH-hohs KEH noh BEHN, koh-rah-SOHN keh noh SYEHN-teh]

(lit: Eyes that don't see, heart that doesn't feel.)

My home is your home.

Mi casa es su casa.

[mee KAH-sah ehs SOO KAH-sah]

Cheers!
or Bless you!
(after a sneeze)

¡Salud!

[sah-LOOD]

(lit: Health!)

I have a terrible
hangover!

¡Tengo tremenda cruda!

[TEHN-goh treh-MEHN-dah KROO-dah]

You're making a
mountain out of
a molehill!

¡Estás haciendo de una pulga un elefante!

[ehs-TAHS ah-SYEHN-doh deh OO-nah
POOL-gah OON eh-leh-FAHN-teh]

(lit: You're making an elephant
out of a flea!)

It's not worth the trouble

No vale la pena.

[noh BAH-leh lah PEH-nah]

You have no shame!

¡No tienes verguenza!

[noh TYEH-nehs behr-GWEHN-sah]

That can't be!

¡No puede ser!

[noh PWEH-deh SEHR]

It's as plain as day!

¡Más claro, ni el agua!

[mahs KLAH-roh, NEE ehl AH-gwah]

(lit: Not even water is this clear!)

How wonderful!

¡Que maravilla!

[KEH mah-rah-VEE-yah]

Every dog has his day!

¡A cada santo le llega su fiesta!

[ah KAH-dah SAHN-toh
leh YEH-gah soo FYEHS-tah]

(lit: Every saint gets his holiday!)

Better late than never.

Más vale tarde que nunca.

[mahs BAH-leh TAHR-deh keh NOON-kah]

I'm joking!

¡Estoy bromeando!

[ehs-TOY broh-meh-AHN-doh]

I've had it up to here!

¡Estoy hasta el copete!

[ehs-TOY AHS-tah ehl koh-PEH-teh]

Like father, like son.

*De tal palo,
tal astilla.*

[DEH tahl PAH-loh, TAHL ahs-TEE-yah]

(lit: From such a stick,
such a splinter.)

It's better than nothing!

¡Peor es nada!

[peh-OHR ehs NAH-dah]

I don't believe it!

¡No me digas!

[NOH meh DEE-gahs]

(lit: Don't tell me!)

Of course!

¡Por supuesto!

[POHR soo-Pwehs-toh]

Bottoms up!

¡Arriba, abajo, al centro, pa'dentro!

[ah-RREE-bah ah-BAH-hoh
ahl SEHN-troh pah-DEHN-troh]

(lit: Up, down, to the
middle, inside!)

It can't last forever.

No hay mal que cien años dure.

[noh eye MAHL keh SYEN AH-nyohs
DOO-reh]

(lit: Nothing bad lasts
a hundred years.)

That's life!

¡Así es la vida!

[ah-SEE ehs la VEE-dah]

Have a nice trip!

¡Buen viaje!

[bwehn BYAH-heh]

Congratulations!

¡Felicidades!

[feh-lee-see-DAH-dehs]